Delaware

Jim Ollhoff

Visit us at
www.abdopublishing.com

Editor: John Hamilton
Graphic Design: Sue Hamilton
Cover Illustration: Neil Klinepier
Cover Photo: mikebiggsphotography.com
Interior Photo Credits: Alamy, AP Images, Beverly Vealach, Corbis, David Listemaa, David Olson, Delaware Geological Survey, DuPont, Getty, Granger Collection, Hale-Byrnes House, iStock Photo, Library of Congress, Mile High Maps, Mountain High Maps, North Wind Picture Archives, One Mile Up Maps, Penn Treaty Museum, Red Cross, Rob Brooks, Seth Gaines, Tim Kiser, U.S. Air Force/Jason Minto and Roland Balik, U.S. Congress, and the U.S. Department of Defense/Bruce Trombecky.
Statistics: State population statistics taken from 2008 U.S. Census Bureau estimates. City and town population statistics taken from July 1, 2007, U.S. Census Bureau estimates. Land and water area statistics taken from 2000 Census, U.S. Census Bureau.

Manufactured with paper containing at least 10% post-consumer waste

Library of Congress Cataloging-in-Publication Data

Ollhoff, Jim, 1959-
  Delaware / Jim Ollhoff.
      p. cm. -- (The United States)
  Includes index.
  ISBN 978-1-60453-643-0
  1. Delaware--Juvenile literature. I. Title.

  F164.3.O44 2010
  975.1--dc22
                          2008051028

Table of Contents

The First State

Delaware has a long history. Native American tribes lived in Delaware for thousands of years. Europeans came in the 1630s. Delaware played an important role in the birth of the United States, and helped the nation grow.

Delaware is a small state, but it is rich in farming, manufacturing, and tourism. One famous United States company has been in Delaware for 200 years. It is DuPont, a maker of chemicals and medicines.

Delaware's nickname is "The First State." In 1783, the United States' original 13 colonies won the American War of Independence against Great Britain. A few years later, leaders created a set of laws called the United States Constitution. Delaware became the first official state when it approved the Constitution on December 7, 1787.

The Harbor of Refuge lighthouse sits at the Delaware Bay entrance. Built more than 100 years ago, it is the only working lighthouse on Delaware's coast.

Quick Facts

DECEMBER 7, 1787

Name: The state is named in honor of Thomas West (1577–1618). He was an English nobleman whose title was "the Baron De La Warr."

State Capital: Dover, population 35,811

Date of Statehood: December 7, 1787 (1st state)

Population: 873,092 (45th-most populous state)

Area (Total Land and Water): 2,489 square miles (6,447 sq km), the 49th-largest state

Largest City: Wilmington, population 72,868

Nickname: The First State

Motto: Liberty and Independence

State Bird: Blue Hen Chicken

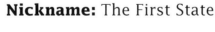

Sillimanite

American Holly

State Flower: Peach Blossom

State Mineral: Sillimanite

State Tree: American Holly

State Song: "Our Delaware"

Highest Point: Ebright Azimuth, 448 feet (137 m)

Lowest Point: Atlantic Ocean, 0 feet (0 m)

Average July Temperature: 74°F (23°C)

Record High Temperature: 110°F (43°C), Millsboro, July 21, 1930

Average January Temperature: 38°F (3°C)

Record Low Temperature: -17°F (-27°C), Millsboro, July 17, 1893

Average Annual Precipitation: 45 inches (114 cm)

Number of U.S. Senators: 2

Number of U.S. Representatives: 1

U.S. Postal Service Abbreviation: DE

Geography

Delaware is the second-smallest state. Only Rhode Island is smaller. Delaware has only three counties.

Most of Delaware is on the Delmarva Peninsula. A peninsula is land that has water on three sides. The Delmarva Peninsula has Delaware on the east side. Maryland is on the west side. A part of Virginia is on the very south part of the peninsula.

Delaware is about 95 miles (153 km) long, from north to south. It is only about 9 miles (14 km) wide in the north. In the southern part of the state, it is about 35 miles (56 km) across.

Delaware Bay is an inlet of water east of Delaware and west of New Jersey. The most southern part of Delaware borders the Atlantic Ocean.

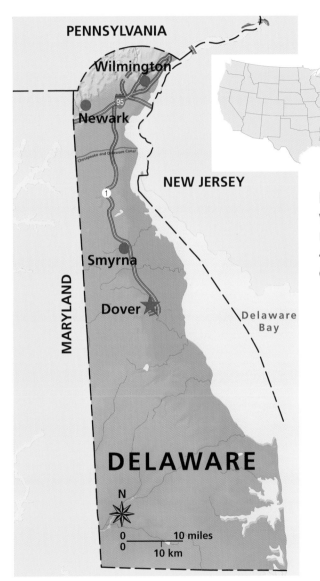

PENNSYLVANIA

Wilmington

Newark

95

Chesapeake and Delaware Canal

NEW JERSEY

1

MARYLAND

Smyrna

Dover

Delaware Bay

DELAWARE

N

0   10 miles
0   10 km

Delaware's total land and water area is 2,489 square miles (6,447 sq km). It is the 49th-largest state. The state capital is Dover.

The Chesapeake and Delaware Canal is a river of water that goes across the Delmarva Peninsula. It is about 14 miles (23 km) long. It cuts across Maryland and Delaware. It makes it much easier for ships from Baltimore, Maryland, to travel to the ocean. The canal is partly natural, but it has been deepened, widened, and straightened by construction projects.

North of the Chesapeake and Delaware Canal, it is mostly urban and industrial. South of the canal is largely agricultural land.

The northern boundary of Delaware is very unusual. Many states have boundaries that are straight, or follow the path of a river. But Delaware's northern boundary is a half-circle. It is measured by a 12-mile (19-km) arc from the courthouse in the town of New Castle.

Ships travel through the Chesapeake and Delaware Canal.

Climate and Weather

The climate of Delaware is humid, which means there is a lot of water vapor in the air. The high humidity is caused by the nearby Atlantic Ocean. Average summer temperatures in Delaware are 80 degrees Fahrenheit (27°C) and higher.

The Atlantic Ocean brings high humidity to Delaware.

In winter, mountains in Pennsylvania protect Delaware from the cold northern winds. The Atlantic Ocean also keeps the winters in Delaware from getting too cold.

Delaware receives about 20 inches (51 cm) of snowfall per year.

Average snowfall is light. For the year, only about 20 inches (51 cm) of snow falls. Winter temperatures range from 31 degrees Fahrenheit (-1°C) in the north to 38 degrees Fahrenheit (3°C) in the south.

Droughts are uncommon. Thunderstorms often happen in the summertime.

Plants and Animals

Before Europeans settled Delaware in the 1600s and 1700s, most of the land was forest. Much of it was cut down for lumber or fuel. The forest was also cleared to make room for farmland. Today, about one-third of Delaware is forest. Common trees include oak, beech, maple, hickory, and ash. Loblolly pines are found in the southern forests. Pitch pines, red cedars, and bayberry trees grow along the coast. Bald cypress trees are found in the Great Cypress Swamp on the southern edge of Delaware.

Common animals found in the state are deer, raccoons, foxes, skunks, and opossums. Smaller animals include rabbits, chipmunks, squirrels, and moles.

A horseshoe crab makes tracks on a beach on Delaware Bay.

Red-Throated Hummingbird

Fiddler Crab

Deer

In Delaware Bay, crabs and clams are harvested. Bluefish, flounder, Norfolk spot, and perch are also found in Delaware Bay. The weakfish is found all along the Atlantic Coast. It is the state fish of Delaware. Bass, pike, and trout live in the ponds and streams of the state.

Weakfish

Snapping turtles are found in swampy areas. The poisonous copperhead snake lives in the state, along with blackrat, hognose, and garter snakes.

Many different kinds of birds live in Delaware. Robins, starlings, cardinals, blue jays, and ruby-throated hummingbirds are common. Along the shore, common birds include great blue herons, sandpipers, gulls, terns, and snowy egrets.

Snapping turtles are found in swampy areas in Delaware.

History

Before Europeans settled Delaware in the 1600s, the land was occupied by Native American tribes. The Lenni Lenape Indians, later called the Delaware Indians, lived in the north and central part of the state. The Minqua lived in the western part of the

Chief Tammany of the Lenni Lenape (Delaware) tribe.

state. The Nanticoke, Assateague, and Choptank tribes lived in the south part of the state. When the Europeans came, the Native Americans moved westward to escape disease and warfare.

Henry Hudson

Spanish and Portuguese explorers probably sailed along the Delaware coast in the late 1500s. The first European that we know for certain sailed near Delaware was Henry Hudson. He was an English explorer working for the Dutch East India Company.

Hudson sailed partway up the Delaware River in 1609. In following years, several other explorers mapped the coast. In 1631, the Dutch tried to start a settlement near today's town of Lewes, Delaware. However, they fought with local Native American tribes, and the settlement was destroyed.

Swedish colonists bring in a harvest in Delaware.

Delaware's first permanent settlement was founded by people from Sweden. They formed Fort Christina in 1638, in the area that would later become the city of Wilmington. That settlement was taken over by the Dutch in 1655. About 10 years later, the English took the fort from the Dutch. Finally, a Pennsylvanian leader named William Penn took over. He allowed Delaware to have its own leadership and government.

In 1776, Delaware adopted its own set of laws, called a constitution. That same year, the 13 American colonies voted to become independent of Great Britain. A new nation was born.

The British did not want the colonies to be independent. This led to the Revolutionary War. About 4,000 Delaware men fought for the colonies. The British army occupied Wilmington, Delaware, during the war. The British navy was stationed in Delaware Bay.

British and Hessian (German) soldiers of the American Revolutionary War.

The Americans officially won the Revolutionary War in 1783. On December 7, 1787, Delaware became the first state to approve the United States Constitution.

Business and industry grew throughout Delaware in the 1800s. The state had many rivers that were used to run machinery.

In 1787, Delaware became the first state to approve the United States Constitution.

Delaware had good access to the Atlantic Ocean. Philadelphia, Pennsylvania, was an easy trip up the Delaware River. The Chesapeake and Delaware Canal opened in 1829. The canal allowed access to the cities of Baltimore, Maryland, and Washington, D.C.

Railroads came through the state in 1838. That made trade and business even easier.

In the 1860s, the state was divided over slavery. Slavery was one of the causes of the Civil War. Delaware did not join the Southern states, which together were called the Confederacy. However, some men from Delaware did join the Confederate army.

An American tanker built in Wilmington, Delaware, in 1915.

After World War I, Delaware had many population shifts, with new immigrants coming from several foreign countries. After World War II, many people moved to Wilmington and its suburbs. In the 1980s, the Delaware government passed laws making it easier for financial companies to work in the state. Many companies moved to Delaware, which greatly helped the economy.

Delaware's Thomas Garrett helped slaves escape.

Delaware's **Thomas Garrett** (1789-1871) was an important stationmaster for the Underground Railroad. He was a Pennsylvanian who moved to Wilmington, Delaware, before the Civil War. This was a time when many African American people were slaves. The nation was fiercely divided on the issue.

When Garrett was young, he came home to terrible news. A free black woman who was employed by his family had been kidnapped. She was taken to be sold into slavery.

Thomas Garrett chased the kidnappers, and then forced them to free the woman. This event made Garrett dedicate his life to stopping slavery.

After moving to Wilmington, Delaware, Garrett began helping with the Underground Railroad. It wasn't really a railroad. It was called "underground" because it was a secret set of routes that people took to escape slavery. Usually, people from the South would get rescued, and walk at night through the countryside to one of the Northern states. They used railroad terms as code. "Stationmasters" hid slaves in their homes. The guides who led the slaves to freedom were called "conductors."

Thomas Garrett was a stationmaster. He hid many escaped slaves in his home. He provided clothing, food, shoes, money, and supplies to the escaped slaves. Garrett was a friend and helper of Harriet Tubman, a very famous conductor. Garrett said he helped about 2,700 slaves find freedom.

People

Joe Biden (1942-) was born in Pennsylvania, but moved to Delaware when he was 10 years old. He attended school in the state, and graduated from the University of Delaware in 1965. He went on to become a lawyer, working in his own law firm in Wilmington. At the age of 29, Biden was elected United States senator for Delaware. He became an expert in foreign policy, as well as leading the way on issues such as terrorism, drugs, crime, and women's rights. He served as Delaware's senator for 36 years. In 2009, he became vice president of the United States, serving with President Barack Obama.

Eleuthère-Irénée du Pont (1771–1834) was born in France. He came to America in about 1799. American gunpowder was poor quality at that time. Du Pont started a gunpowder plant near Wilmington that produced very good gunpowder. His gunpowder became important in the War of 1812. His company became very successful. In later years, it produced many different kinds of chemicals. Du Pont died near Greenville in 1834.

Annie Jump Cannon (1863-1941) was an astronomer, a scientist who studies the stars. She was born and grew up in Dover. She helped to create a way of categorizing stars according to their temperature, called the Harvard Classification Scheme. She won many honors for her work. Her career is even more remarkable because she was almost completely deaf.

Caesar Rodney (1728-1784) was a statesman and a signer of the Declaration of Independence. He was born near Dover, Delaware. He served many political and military duties. In 1776, the nation voted for its independence from England. Caesar Rodney rode by horseback all night to Philadelphia, Pennsylvania, in time to cast Delaware's vote for independence. He was appointed general of the Delaware militia in 1777, and became governor in 1778. He died shortly after his term ended.

Emily Bissell (1861-1948) was born in Wilmington, Delaware. At the age of 15, she began doing volunteer work to help others. This mission to help others would carry her throughout her life. She helped to provide the first free kindergarten in Wilmington. She also worked to help immigrants who were new to the United States.

In the early 1900s, she began to work for doctors who treated tuberculosis, a disease of the lungs. It was a dangerous disease in those days, and there was little funding to help. She created a stamp that would make people aware of the disease. At first, she sold the stamps at local post offices. Eventually, these "Christmas Seals" raised a huge amount of money in the fight against tuberculosis.

Cities

Wilmington is the largest city in Delaware. It has a population of 72,868. Settlers from Sweden first came to the Wilmington area in 1638. It was captured by the Dutch in 1655. The English captured it in 1664. It became an important port town when the Quakers moved in during the 1730s. In 1802, Frenchman Eleuthère-Irénée du Pont began a gunpowder mill. Sawmills and flour mills were also established. In the 1830s, the railroads came through and the city grew quickly. Today, Wilmington is still a center for manufacturing, but the city also contains many finance companies and other businesses.

Dover is the capital of Delaware. It is located in the central part of the state. William Penn, a leader in the state of Pennsylvania, helped to organize Dover in 1683. It was officially laid out as a city in 1717. Today, it contains many historic buildings. It is a popular tourist spot.

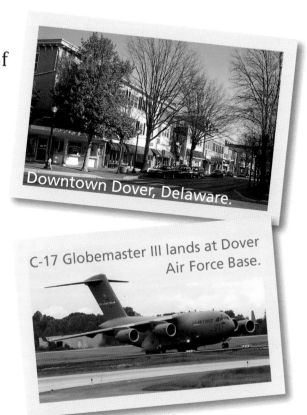

Downtown Dover, Delaware.

C-17 Globemaster III lands at Dover Air Force Base.

Dover is the home of Delaware State University and Wesley College. Nearby, Dover Air Force Base is an important military center. The population of Dover is 35,811.

Newark began in the 1680s, centered around a Quaker house that was open for travelers. In the mid-1700s, another historic home was built by local man Warwick Hale. On September 6, 1777, General George Washington met

Hale-Byrnes House

with several officers of the Continental army in this brick house. In 1798, a paper mill opened. Today, the city continues its manufacturing industries with concrete, automobiles, and processed foods. The population is 29,992. The city is the home of the University of Delaware.

A student at the University of Delaware in Newark.

Smyrna has a population of 8,223. It is in the central part of the state. Although people lived in the Smyrna area since the early 1700s, the city was actually founded in the 1750s. It was first named Duck Creek. In 1806, the name of the town was changed to Smyrna, which is a city mentioned in the Bible. Smyrna has maintained a number of historic buildings.

Smyrna, Delaware, has a lot of classic and historic buildings such as the town's high school, bank, and fire station.

Transportation

One interstate goes through Delaware. Interstate 95 goes through Wilmington in between Philadelphia, Pennsylvania, and Baltimore, Maryland. Most of the traffic in Delaware is between Wilmington and its suburbs. There are more than 6,000 miles (9,656 km) of public roads. The cities of Baltimore, Washington, D.C., and Philadelphia are all within a two-hour drive of Wilmington.

The first railroad in Delaware was built in the 1830s. About 230 miles (370 km) of railroads are still in use today. Railroads ship mostly freight and chemicals.

Wilmington is a large port on the Atlantic Coast. A lot of traffic goes back and forth on the Chesapeake and Delaware Canal.

The biggest public airport in Delaware is New Castle Airport. A very important military air base is Dover Air Force Base.

An airman signals in a C-17 Globemaster III at Dover Air Force Base.

Natural Resources

There are about 2,200 farms in Delaware. Soybeans and corn are the most important crops. Farmers also grow a small amount of potatoes, wheat, peas, apples, and peaches.

Many chickens are raised in Delaware. Chickens make up about 90 percent of the state's livestock income. Pigs are raised mostly in the southwest. There are also a few farms that raise turkeys and cattle.

In the Atlantic Ocean and in Delaware Bay, the fishing industry hauls in almost seven million dollars of product every year. This is mostly from crabs, but they also catch clams, oysters, and sea trout.

Most of the mining in the state is for gravel and sand. Companies also do a small amount of lumbering.

A woman stands in a barn full of chickens at a Delaware farm. Chickens make up about 90 percent of the state's livestock income.

Industry

Delaware is close to many major cities along the East Coast. Because of this, Delaware has become a manufacturing center to supply these cities. Manufacturing is a big part of Delaware's

DuPont's World Headquarters is in Wilmington, Delaware.

economy. The major manufactured products include transportation equipment and chemicals. Chemicals manufactured in Delaware include paint, medicines, and dyes. Food, paper, plastics, and electronic products are also important to the economy. Most of the industry is in the Wilmington area.

Delaware passed laws that made it easier for banks to do business in the state. State leaders created courts that can understand complex financial issues. So, Delaware has become a center for finance and banking. Many foreign countries have businesses in Delaware.

The southern part of Delaware has more wildlife areas and ocean resorts. Many tourists enjoy the historic buildings located throughout the state.

Both local residents and visitors enjoy Delaware's Rehoboth Beach.

Sports

Delaware has no major-league professional football, baseball, basketball, or hockey teams. However, the state has several minor-league teams. Many people

in Delaware follow nearby sports teams in Baltimore, Philadelphia, or Washington, D.C. The University of Delaware sports teams are also popular.

The University of Delaware's lacrosse team has been in several playoff games.

Delaware also has had sports teams in women's professional football, women's soccer, and roller derby. Delaware hosts NASCAR races, horse racing, and some professional wrestling tournaments.

There are many outdoor activities in the state. Boating, swimming, and fishing are all popular. There are many state parks and forests where people can hike or watch wildlife. Redden State Forest, in the southern part of the state, is the largest of the state parks.

Fishing boats near the Harbor of Refuge Light at Cape Henlopen, Delaware.

Entertainment

One of the attractions in Delaware are the old historic buildings that have been preserved. Some historic buildings were constructed as far back as the late 1600s. The Holy Trinity (Old Swedes) Church in Wilmington dates back to 1698. It is a National Historic Landmark. The Old Dutch House in New Castle dates to around 1700.

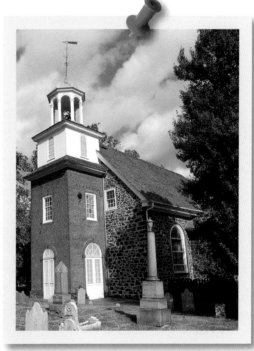

Wilmington's Holy Trinity Church is the nation's oldest church building still standing as originally built. It is also known as Old Swedes Church. The church was constructed from 1698-1699.

There are many museums in Delaware as well. Some are museums

The Delaware Museum of Natural History.

that help people understand history, like the Delaware Museum of Natural History, or the Henry Francis du Pont Winterthur Museum. Other museums showcase art, such as the Hagly Museum and the Delaware Art Museum, both in Wilmington.

The Delaware State Fair is held every July in the city of Harrington. Old Dover Days celebrates the historic homes in the city of Dover. The city of Odessa is home to the Delaware Decoy Festival every October. It has a carving contest for decoys that are used in duck hunting.

Timeline

Pre-1600s—The Delaware, Minqua, Nanticoke, Assateague, and Choptank Native American tribes live in Delaware.

Henry Hudson

1609—Explorer Henry Hudson sails part way up the Delaware River.

1631—The Dutch settle near the modern-day city of Lewes.

1638—A Swedish colony is established at Fort Christina, in modern-day Wilmington.

Peter Stuyvesant

1651—Dutch governor Peter Stuyvesant establishes Fort Casimir at modern-day New Castle.

William Penn

1655—The Dutch take over the Swedish colony at Fort Christina.

1682—William Penn takes over the leadership of Delaware.

1787—Delaware becomes the first state to ratify the United States Constitution.

1802—DuPont Powder Mill is built on the banks of Brandywine Creek near Wilmington, Delaware.

1941—The beginning of World War II for the United States. Construction begins on Dover Air Force Base.

Joe Biden

2009—Joe Biden, former Delaware senator, is sworn in as vice president of the U.S.

Glossary

Chesapeake and Delaware Canal—A waterway that cuts across part of Maryland and Delaware. It leads from Chesapeake Bay to Delaware Bay. The canal makes it much easier for ships going to and from Baltimore, Maryland, to connect to Wilmington, Delaware, and Philadelphia, Pennsylvania, or the Atlantic Ocean.

Civil War—The war fought between America's Northern and Southern states from 1861-1865. The Southern states were for slavery. They wanted to start their own country. Northern states fought against slavery and a division of the country.

Colony—A group of people who settle in a distant territory but remain citizens of their native country.

Delmarva Peninsula—The peninsula where Delaware is located. The Delmarva Peninsula also is home to parts of Maryland and Virginia.

Lenni Lenape Indians—A Native American tribe that lived in Delaware before the arrival of the Europeans. The Europeans later named this tribe the "Delaware Indians."

Militia—A group of citizens enrolled in military service during a time of emergency.

Peninsula—An area of land with water on three sides.

Quaker—A member of the Religious Society of Friends. Quakers are a Christian group that was founded in 1650 by George Fox.

Revolutionary War—The war fought between the American colonies and Great Britain from 1775-1783. It is also known as the American Revolution or the War of Independence.

World War I—A war that was fought in Europe from 1914 to 1918, involving countries around the world. The United States entered the war in April 1917.

World War II—A conflict across the world, lasting from 1939-1945. The United States entered the war in December 1941.

Index